# Can We Keep Him?

*A Collection of Dog Poems*

## Nancy Taylor

## About the Author

Nancy Taylor is a retired nurse practitioner who spent 30 years in a wide variety of nursing positions. She now lives on Bainbridge Island with her husband and two dogs where she enjoys writing, gardening, hiking and volunteering with RESULTS, a citizen advocacy group that aims to end extreme poverty in the U.S. and globally. She began studying poetry in 2010 with Kay Mullen's Inscape Poets in Tacoma, WA. Four of her poems were published in that group's anthology, *Women Writing: on the Edge of Dark and Light*. Others have appeared in *Poetry Corners 2017* and in *Ars Poetica 2016* and *2017*. This is Nancy's debut book.

First published 2018

www.blurb.com/user/NancyJTaylor

fb.me/NancyTaylorPoetry | nancyjtaylorpoetry@gmail.com

Illustrations by Nancy Taylor

"One must have the mind of dogs" and "Hydrotherapy"
illustrations by Erin Walsh

Book design, book cover, "Future Dog Tales" illustration by Andrea Sullivan

*This book is dedicated to shelter workers
and to the animals who need homes.*

To be blessed
said the dog
is to have a pinch
of God
inside you
and all the other dogs
can smell it.

**Alicia Suskin Ostriker**

# Contents

## "Can we keep him?"

begs my brother when
an Irish Setter follows him home
from Dairy Queen.
Our parents say, "This dog belongs
to someone," so they post a notice.

The owner shows, looks us over,
says, "The place I'm renting
won't allow dogs.
Can you buy him?
I'll bring his papers by—
his name's Patrick."
We feel sorry
for the sad, young man

but celebrate after he leaves
and give the dog a last name.
Dad builds a kennel and doghouse
where Patrick O'Shannessy sleeps
though we bring him in to watch TV—
use him for a pillow.

# Homeless

Shivering, disheveled and wet,
he hides
under an overturned
table behind the bankrupt
Sea Grill Restaurant,
surviving on cast-off
chicken wings
from a nearby pub.

Downtown Tacoma crowds
pass the orphaned puppy
to board a trolley.
He quivers at its jangle
and the clamor of cars
zooming
off the freeway.

One drizzly day
a passing couple
spot the trembling
terrier. They pause.
Their gaze connects—
a decision made.

# Yankee Doodle Dandy

His pedigree:
Shih Tsu + Lhasa Apso = Shih Apso.
All shades of beige,
he looks like a Shih Tsu
on bowed stilts.

While his story is a dandy,
I suspect the name
comes from his 4th of July birthdate.

When he was 6 weeks old,
Millie found the puppy
trapped in a filthy laundry room
lacking food and water.
Millie agreed to his "temporary care"
and named him Dandy.

Now, 11 years later,
she gets him groomed monthly,
gives him blood pressure pills
twice a day and walks him
every morning.

Although Millie would like
to move, Dandy's blood pressure
spiked and left him blind.
So she considers:
here he knows his way around,
he's familiar with the placement
of furniture and smells
of paths in the park.

## Good Friday in
## Heredia, Costa Rica

Where town square meets
cathedral steps, a small brown dog
lies panting on the pavement
as if waiting for the procession
of Christ's image to arrive
at its final station.

I ask people
resting in nearby shade
if they know the dog's owner.

When they deny knowing,
I ponder Peter's denial of Christ,
then offer her water
in a paper cup.

## Dog on the Move

At the pound in Dodgeville, Wisconsin
      (home of Land's End)
my brother's family finds a puppy,
so they tote the terrier home
      to share their sofa as they root
for the Badgers. They name
      their nine-month-old,
mottled-brown, toy terrier Maxie.
Two years later an oil boom draws

Maxie's family to the North Dakota plains,
where his whiskers wear frost in winter,
      where inflatable boots
keep his feet from freezing
      and prairie winds gust year-round.
Before being blown away,

they move to mountainous Flagstaff
where you can follow your nose
to the Purina Dog Chow plant
      east of town.
Just as Maxie adjusts to the altitude,

they transfer to San Luis Obispo
where he sheds winter gear,
      scampers on the beach,
and explores Morro Bay.
Here the land truly ends
      and the fleas never freeze.

## Inky's First Bath

Maybe it was the introduction
to warm, sudsy water
flowing over his back

or maybe it was the tubfuls
of filthy water chasing his garbage
smell down the drain

or maybe it was the first time
anyone handled him gently
that began the bond.

# Like Clockwork

At 18 months a white and brown
  beagle/Jack Russell terrier
   with distemper, was trucked
    from Modesto to Seattle where
   a vet nurtured her to health

then found her a forever home
 with my friend who named
  her Sophie. Now, age 9,
   she's walked every morning,
    eats when she's hungry,

and gets proper petting.
 Nightly, at 10 o'clock on the dot,
  an alarm in Sophie's head
   says it's time for bed
    so she hops off the couch

and goes out the house to pee.
 Upon her return she scampers
  straight to her brown, plaid
   bed without even
    wagging *goodnight*.

## Our Skippersetter

From overcoat pockets
our neighbor plucked two tiny puppies
and said, "Keep them awhile...
choose one."
Our parents were less excited
than we kids

but after a week
our choice was unanimous—
a spunky, black furball
we named Sparky—
his dam a small, black Skipperkie,
his sire an Irish Setter.

Smart like his mother
and thrice her size,
our 36-pound dog
pointed out prey
with a Setter profile
So we dubbed him a "Skippersetter."
When he was young, a car ran over him

without leaving a scar,
but the scare remained.
When we got locked out
Sparky would pry a dowel
from the sliding glass door track
to let us in.

If he too was locked out
we'd hoist him through
the kitchen window
where he'd shimmy past the sink,
jump to the floor
to pry the dowel.

Every school day, Sparky took
a running jump up a leaning willow
where he wedged between boughs
to watch for us.

In the no-leash-law-'60's,
Sparky ran free.
If he was "dating" he'd take off
for a few days.
I'd worry,
but he always returned home
where his toenails clicked across
hardwood floors.

When the time came
to say goodbye
I'd moved far away.
Still, on return visits
I'd listen for Sparky's
click across the floor.

## Tucker Keeps His Cool

At the Humane Society
Sue chooses a strawberry-blond,
blue-tongued chow-chow
she names Tucker.

His double-coat steels him
to Minnesota cold,
and long walks
seal their bond.

Tucker only barks
when the cat wants in,
a pumpkin's smashed,
or a prowler pokes about.

Sue admires
his fearlessness with fireworks,
his mildness when a dachshund
nips him in the belly,
and his restraint
when her cat implants
a claw in his nose.

## Othello

A Great Dane
nudges his head
under my hand to prompt
a good boy greeting—
slobbering just a little.

Pestered by insecurity,
like his namesake,
this powerful rescue dog
sleeps with blanket
and stuffed animals.

Leaning his 140 pounds
on me, his short, black fur
and scent rub off.

Othello's unconcerned that
my dog Justin's at home
waiting to sniff hints
of my whereabouts.

## Patrick O'Shannessy

When he doesn't retrieve ducks
we think he's not too bright.
But that's O.K., he's handsome,
so I paint his toenails hot pink
and my brother freaks—
"You ruined my dog."

Apparently the shade
doesn't compliment
his auburn coat.

## Cece, our new leash-naive dog,

meanders across my path.
Sometimes her leash
crosses over
my other dog's leash,
so I switch hands
or twist around
to avoid getting ensnarled.

After watching us
unentangle, our neighbor Bob,
contrives a leash that
forks with a rotating toggle,
which functions swimmingly
until my son's dog, Inky,
joins our parade.

## *Your Dog's Smarter*

I once regarded my dogs
as intelligent.
They would sit, shake, stay,
and leave it on command.

Then, my son rescued
a terrier mix
who decodes spelling.

So W-A-L-K when his owners
consider a walk,
has changed to K-L-A-W

for now.

## *Old Yeller naps on his driveway*

catching slanted, late day rays
till awakened by
a small knight-errant
throwing down the gauntlet,
barking, back legs braced.

The yellow lab looks up, sees
the yappy little Havanese,
yawns, then lays
his head back down.
The little dog must prove
his chivalry elsewhere.

# Cece Barks Like a Dog

I consider testing my dog's
DNA to see if she's a cat.
Aloof like Annie Hall

she's uninterested in pleasing me
and her favorite pastime
is chasing birds.

When my neighbor fed her
cat food she scarfed it down—
didn't even get a little sick.

Not only am I curious about
the code in her double helixes—
I'm also allergic to cats.

# Behavior Modification

Since Cece, our 9-pound Havanese,
is afraid of people and dogs,
my husband and I attend
a dog anxiety class. We consider
her brother, Justin, well-adjusted until
the instructor shares a list of behaviors
we recognize in him too.

As behavior modification techniques
are taught, I yawn repeatedly.
The more I try to stop, the more I yawn.
Realizing the effort entailed to correct
my imperfect dogs,
I become narcoleptic.

Homework involves journaling actions
that precede incessant barking—
licking, chewing on body parts,
perking ears.
I nudge my husband,
tell him he needs to "notice" better,
then hand him the journal and nod off.

## Yoga Lessons

Each morning
after Cody climbs from his bed
he stretches
in a hybrid
"down dog/child's pose"
elongating his spine
before he dashes
downstairs.

After shuffling
from his bed in the daytime
he stretches again,
opening his Third Eye chakra,
which helps him intuit
when he'll get
a treat.

Sometimes he stands
in a "tabletop pose,"
drawing earth energy
up through his paws.

## Gardening Trials

Because my solar-powered owl
  stops rotating its head—
    undaunted chickadees steal seeds.

      Because blueberries
        begin to ripen—
          flickers taunt from my fence.

        Because robins scoff while hopping
          from post to post—
            worms drop from beaks.

          Because my white dogs
            just got groomed—
              they roll in dead worms.

            Because I top crops
              with compost—
                dogs dig and ingest.

# Not Mother's Housekeeping

Since my house is looking shaggy,
I begin scouring the bathroom
and consider—
*can new technology possibly
keep porcelain toilets
"cleaner, longer"
as its box proclaims?*

My vacuum, a Dyson, requires
frequent emptying since fur
from my "non-shedding dogs"
mixes with broken bits
of kibble Cece drags
throughout the house.
(She's a social eater.)

On to the kitchen where
appliances flaunt fingerprints
like rock stars flash tats.
Here my dogs lick the floor
fairly clean. I remember
what a chore it was for Mom
to scrub, then wax her floors.

Her dogs must have been
slackers.

## Almost Busted

On sunny days,
Inky digs under the fence
to canvas
the neighborhood.

Returning home
one afternoon,
he sees the woman
who'd been chasing him
waiting on the porch.
So he hides and waits.

Inky's human arrives home
to learn that a neighbor
had lodged a complaint.
He tells the dogcatcher,
"My dog can't get loose,"
then points to another house
where a small terrier lives.

When the dogcatcher leaves,
Inky scurries up the driveway,
tail wagging.

# My Friend's Dog

Not her elegant brindle coat,
nor her sleek physique
but her

     rare barking
     calm greeting of owners
     coming when called
     not begging at the table

wows me.

I'm going home to put
my dogs on notice
no more

     incessant barking
     jumping on me when I come home
     hiding under chairs at walk-time
     begging at the table.

They can thank Skittles
for the new rules.

## Reading his Blog

Gingerly, Justin smells several
         blades in a tuft of grass
then marks a particular
         spot as territory.

En route, he pauses to sniff points
         of interest. Does he recognize
a familiar scent, who's in heat
         or who's ill?

Today, he's permitted time to read
         his "dog blog."
Tail wagging—
         he deciphers a message.

# Thirteen Ways of Looking at a Dog

after "Thirteen Ways of Looking at a Blackbird"
by Wallace Stevens

I
Among a neighborhood
of backyards,
the only moving thing
was the eye of a dog.

II
I was of two minds,
like a backyard
in which there are two dogs.

III
The dog chased his tail
in the post-rain air.
It was "act one" of the charade.

IV
"A man and a woman are one.
A man and a woman and a dog
are one."

V
I do not know which to prefer—
the appeal of the obvious
or the appeal of allusion—
the dog howling
or just after.

VI
Cobwebs filled the corners
with silk filagree.
The shadow of the dog
crossed it, to and fro.
The spirit
forecast in the shadow
an unclear source.

VII
O thin men of Bainbridge
why do you fantasize about
golden dogs?
Do you not see how the dog
walks about the feet
of the women around you?

VIII
I know high-born accents
and bawdy street slang;
but I also know,
that the dog intuits
what I know.

IX
As the dog trotted out of view
it marked the perimeter
of one of many fields.

X
At the sight of a pack of dogs
running in green light
even Clark Kent
would shun the phone booth.

XI
He rode across Kitsap County
in an SUV.
Once, a fear seared him,
when he mistook
the shadow of his Subaru
for a pack of dogs.

XII
The river is rushing.
The dog must be running.

XIII
It was gray all day,
it was raining
and would continue to rain.
The dog sat
on the waterlogged lawn.

THE DOGS HAVE THEIR SAY

# My Adjustment

by Inky

What'd I do wrong?
I don't cause trouble
and now I'm boarding
at my cousins' again.

Their kibble is nasty
and I'm not comfortable
eating from their bowl.

Normally on weekdays
I'm home alone.
I like it that way.
Here I lack peace and quiet
but can put up with the hassle
as long as they give me treats,
and rub my belly.

At least I can share their mom,
but I see Justin watching
when she pets me.
He probably wants to kill me.
I know he's into wrestling
but I'm a lover not a fighter.

# Sharing Mom

by Justin

My cousin Inky comes to stay and
Mom gives him attention
she usually showers on me.
I watch her rub his belly
and brush him every day.
My last combing was 8 weeks ago,
before my summer cut.
Now Inky gets a bath.
Can't Mom see
I'm dishwater grey?

I tell myself, "this too shall pass"
his parents always take him back.
At least I still intimidate him
at suppertime. On the other hand,
when he's here we take more walks
and get extra treats
till he settles in.
Maybe he'll wrestle with me.
We're a close match
and he usually lets me win.

# Born to Bark

## by Cece

Before they round the corner I smell dogs,
deer, coyotes, and people, so I bark
to call Mom's attention.
She remains clueless
and may be a little slow.
Doesn't she care we're being stalked?

She hates it when I bark
but boy I went crazy
the other night
when that stranger came slinking
around our house.
My brother and cousin echoed my alarm
and we scared him away for good.
As always, Mom's first response
was to shush me before
she called me a good girl.

I see her reading books
with dogs on the cover
but she still doesn't get me.
Sure she pets me
when my tail's down
and fills my kibble bowl
but all the fuss she makes when I bark
drives me crazy.

# Canine Pointers

Aim to please

Bark to alarm

Come when called

Don't tug on your leash

Eat people food when possible

Follow your nose

Graze on grass to settle your stomach

Heel when walking

Inspect the unusual

Jump for the ball

Kibble-up to quell hunger

Lick your wounds

Mark your trail

Never wander from master

Obey your owner

Pee and poo outdoors

Quench thirst by panting

Rest while waiting

Steer clear of coyotes

Tell feelings with your tail

Use all your senses

Vet strangers

Watch out for cars

Xpcct petting

Yelp if hurt

Zing, your master's home!

# Biology 101

Zoologist Bob and botanist Evan
seated on an auditorium stage
pontificate;
"The strongest, healthiest beings
are genetically jumbled."

Thirty years later,
I buy two purebred Havanese
puppies from a breeder
who said, "Our sires are from Europe
to prevent overbreeding."
Today my dogs cost me a mint—
cardiac echoes to monitor
heart murmurs,
trips to an animal ophthalmologist
for a rare eye disease,
allergy pills a dollar a day.

When my son rescues
a terrier mix from the street,
he proves Bob and Evan's point.

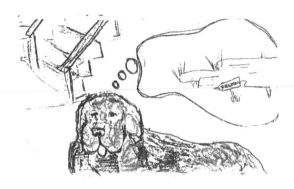

## Hydrotherapy

After adoption from foster care, BearBear.
a one hundred fifty pound Newfoundland,
becomes a computer store mascot

where he rests on a cool, concrete
basement floor as clients shop
the store's showroom. If BearBear hears

a ruckus, he muffles a bark
as he lumbers upstairs to assess
whether his bouncer skills are needed.

Since his knee surgery a year ago
he's not fond of walking,
but give him an icy blue lake...

## Justin, my Havanese, awakens from surgery

to assess his situation—
        bare patch on his foreleg,
        spots shaved on his back,
        sore jaw,
        a missing upper tooth.

Confusion clouds his chocolate eyes
as they search mine. Before this sleep
he was covered with silky, white fur.

Forever the nurse, I want to explain
        I.V. site on his foreleg,
        skin lesions excised,
        cyst removed from his jaw,
        loose tooth extracted.

He licks shaved areas,
scratches sutures, till finally
blue booties
shoe his back paws
and a blue, wide-brim collar
help his skin knit.

Unable to easily scratch, lick, or sniff,
he sleeps away his sentence.

# *Superstitious?*

Cece, my champagne-colored
Havanese, skips—
occasionally favoring
her left hind leg.

While patella subluxation
afflicts such small breeds,
our vet does not detect
a defect.

I count skips,
every 20th, 24th—no,
every 5th step—avoiding her
right hind leg now.

This irregular pattern persists
so the vet reassesses,
then says:
"Patellas are good."

One evening walk,
I notice Cece
only skips over wider
sidewalk cracks.

I too avoided cracks—
just in case.

## *One must have a mind of dogs*

to understand how they
live in the moment
like Buddhist monks,

to understand their quality of life
is heightened by their senses—
       sniffing wet spots,
       tasting bone marrow,
       relishing tummy rubs.

While tails wag
to convey their moods,
don't expect to hide yours—

they get you.

## *Bait*

On today's morning walk
a couple stop to greet us.
We chat about coyotes
in the neighborhood
and they warn
that Cece is eagle bait.

I flash back to a moonless night
taking the dogs out before bed.
A barn owl swooped,
brushed my shoulder—
which altered its course—
and missed Cece
in its scoop.

# The Legend of Teddy

The black lab's first job
began at three months
when he carried in the newspaper.
In time, the deliveryman
tossed the paper
for Teddy to catch.

When a sock dropped
from a laundry basket,
or TV remote was beyond reach,
Teddy was handy.

Once his master dropped
a framing hammer, while dangling
from the roof, Teddy jawed it and
climbed a ladder 5 rungs for delivery.

Trained to bring back,
Teddy did just that
till cancer took him away.

Today, he remains a legend
at Sauvie Island
where hunters watched
him retrieve ducks up to 400 yards.
At times, en route to his quarry,
he broke through ice
like a Coast Guard Cutter.

# An Old Dog

Maximilian greets owners
more dependably than Carson
in Downton Abbey.
His big brown eyes
read their days
before he attends
to his own needs.
Later, lying down, he'll become
the ottoman for their feet.

## *Elegy to Trixie*

Rescued by shelter workers,
eight-week-old puppies
Skittles and Trixie avoid
euthanasia.

Since each whimpers
like a newborn baby
when the other's out of sight
they are crated together
and adopted out as a pair
to a family of four
who hike, jog,
and play fetch with them.

Twelve years later
Trixie succumbs to cancer.
Now, Skittles spends
much of her day in a crate
that's losing Trixie's scent.
She cuddles with a stuffed
brown bear, and carries it
everywhere.

## *Fresh Air*

On a post-rain walk
my dog's nose twitches
like a windshield wiper
to waft scents.

His happy tail prompts
me to inhale deeply.

# Max

Overweight, arthritic, and a tad mangy—
10-year-old Max, a gentle lab mix,
survives outdoors till James
and Danielle adopt him.

When their vet declares him obese,
they ration kibble. Sometimes
toys and socks fill his belly
but exit intact.

Max retrieves his leash
for routine walks and slims down.
Eventually, his hilly neighborhood
tests him so he rests in the road.
His walks shrink to corner mail retrieval.

Now 13, he lumbers
to the front door
to greet whoever's there.
Awkwardly, on fused joints,
he wills himself forward for a pet.
Then, back to bed, head-propped,
his bright eyes study us.

*Should he be put to rest?*
Danielle wonders. She denies
hearing moans or whimpers.
For now we agree—he looks happy.

# Dog Lessons

My dog teaches *concentration*—
out-staring me when our eyes connect

and *patience*—waiting at the window,
undeterred by thirst or hunger.

He models *moderation*—
declining food when sated

and *spontaneity*—
chasing birds that land nearby.

His needs are few—pets, kibble,
and a bed with a ledge to prop his head.

He shows *compassion*—
guarding people who ail

and expresses *forgiveness*—
licking my face after a scolding.

## Release It

When I restrain my over-excited dog
from greeting a fellow canine
walking down the street,
he shakes it off, sniffs a bush.

A lesson I should apply
when grievances
fester in my craw—
beats gnashing teeth
in my dreams.

## Future Dog Tales

By the time you read this—

Cece may grow more dog-like,
Justin may teach me more lessons,
Inky may discover a new escape route,
Skittles may get a new crate-mate,
Othello may forego his blanket,
Sophie may begin bedtime ritual earlier,
Little Maxie may explore a new land,
Cody may master a new pose,
BearBear may lumber to the lake.

Sparky, Patrick, Teddy, Tucker, Trixie
and Max's families will continue
to recall their dogs' quirky
and endearing traits.

# Acknowledgements

I wish to thank Nancy Rekow for her incredible
patience with editing and bird-dogging this effort.

I applaud Andrea Sullivan for formatting,
computer graphics and creative cover art.

Thanks to my sister, Sue Schrader, and her husband,
Dave, for helping me envision my poems as a book.

Gratitude goes to my first poetry mentor, Kay
Mullen, for igniting my love of poetry.

I appreciate friends in poetry groups in Tacoma and
Bainbridge Is. who have lent advice for earlier versions of
these poems. And kudos to David Stallings, Neil Doherty,
and my husband Tom Taylor for editing and encouragement.

Without friends and family who have rescued and
shared dog tales, this book would not have been
written, so thank you for loving your dogs.